First published in Great Britain in 1996 by Brockhampton Press, a member of the
Hodder Headline Group, 20 Bloomsbury Street, London WC1B 3QA.

This series of little gift books was made by Frances Banfield, Kate Brown, Laurel Clark,
Penny Clarke, Clive Collins, Melanie Cumming, Nick Diggory, Deborah Gill, David
Goodman, Douglas Hall, Maureen Hill, Nick Hutchison, John Hybert, Kate Hybert,
Douglas Ingram, Simon London, Patrick McCreeth, Morse Modaberi, Tara Neill, Anne
Newman, Grant Oliver, Michelle Rogers, Nigel Soper, Karen Sullivan and Nick Wells.

Compilation and selection copyright © 1996 Brockhampton Press.

All rights reserved. No part of this publication may be reproduced, stored in a retrieval
system, or transmitted, in any form or by any means, without the prior written
permission of the copyright holder.

ISBN 1 86019 435 4

A copy of the CIP data is available from the British Library upon request.

Produced for Brockhampton Press by Flame Tree Publishing,
a part of The Foundry Creative Media Company Limited,
The Long House, Antrobus Road, Chiswick W4 5HY.

Printed and bound in Italy by L.E.G.O. Spa.

THE LITTLE BOOK OF *Chocolate*

Selected by Beth Hurley

THE LITTLE BOOK OF CHOCOLATE

My desire for chocolate has seldom abated,
even in times of great peril.

Marcel Desaulniers

Chocolate-coated Orange Peel

Dip pieces of candied orange peel
into melted chocolate.
Leave to set.

In the 16th century cocoa beans
were the chief form of currency in
Central America. A rabbit cost 10
beans, and a 'tolerably good' slave
could be had for 100 beans.

I love to eat chocolate.
On Sunday my Daddy won't let
me have chocolate.

Benjamin, 6

Milk chocolate is a yokel taste.

Nieman Marcus, *Quest for the Best*

The Aztec word *xocoatl* means 'bitter water',
which is an apt description of the beverage as the
Aztecs drank it.

There was a young gourmet of Crediton
Who took pâté de foie gras and spread it on
A chocolate biscuit.
He murmured, 'I'll risk it.'
His tomb bears the date that he said it on.

Anonymous

'When I die,' I said to my friend,
'I'm not going to be embalmed,
I'm going to be dipped.'
'Milk chocolate or bittersweet?'
was her immediate concern.

Adrianne Marcus, *The Chocolate Bible*

Chocolates.

"TRY one," said the
  Chocolate Almonds;
"You will find us good to eat;
And we don't mind being eaten
  By a little maid
    so sweet!"

Coo.

"COO," said
  the pretty
pigeons, "coo;
We're not a bit
  afraid of you;
You love us so —
  we know you do,
And no one
  could help
    loving you!"

THE LITTLE BOOK OF CHOCOLATE

Give Chocolates this Season

It's so easy to settle your Gift problems—just visit your confectioner's and ask him to show you Rowntree's beautiful festive boxes. There is sure to be something you would like to give, at a price you wish to pay.

Every Rowntree fancy box is marked underneath with the chocolate assortment it contains. That is your guarantee of quality.

Rowntree's York Chocolates are especially recommended—there is "no charge for the box" on 1-lb. and upwards. The price you pay is the price of the chocolates inside. *Full weight, full value.*

They're right — if they're Rowntree's

YORK CHOCOLATES

For two hundred years after the introduction of chocolate to Europe in the 16th century the controversy raged as to whether it was a food or a drink, and thus whether it was permissible to drink it on the church's feast days.

The unique, melt-in-the-mouth texture and inimitable flavour make good chocolate irresistible to most of us.

Anonymous

Jacob, with pistol in his hand,
exclaims, 'Susannah, dear,
without your love I'll kill myself!'
Susannah quakes in fear.
He lays the pistol to his head,
Susannah pleads, 'Wait, wait!'
'Don't fret!' says Jacob, 'for this gun
is only chocolate!'

Swiss poem, 1840

Chocolate Cheesecake

For the base:
200g crushed chocolate wafers or digestive biscuits
melted butter to mix

For the cake:
500g cream cheese
150g sugar
3 eggs
225g plain chocolate, melted
250ml whipping cream, beaten until thick
1 tbs cocoa powder
1 tsp vanilla essence

Mix the crushed chocolate wafers or digestive biscuits with the melted butter; press into the base of a 22cm springform cake tin and chill.

Blend cream cheese and sugar together. Add eggs, beating. Blend in the melted chocolate, whipped cream,

cocoa powder and vanilla essence. Pour over the base.
Bake at 230°C/450°F/gas mark 8 for 10 minutes,
then reduce temperature to 120°C/250°F/gas mark ½
and bake for a further 35-40 minutes.
Refrigerate overnight or for at least five hours.
Drizzle with melted chocolate before serving.

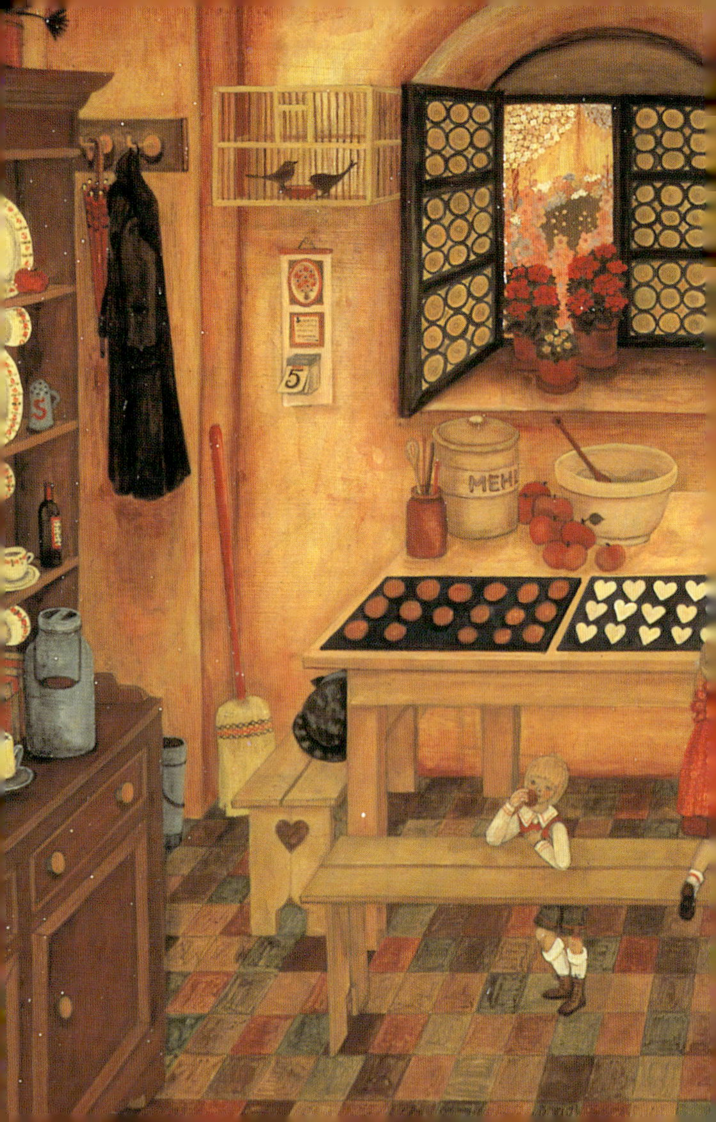

MEHL
5

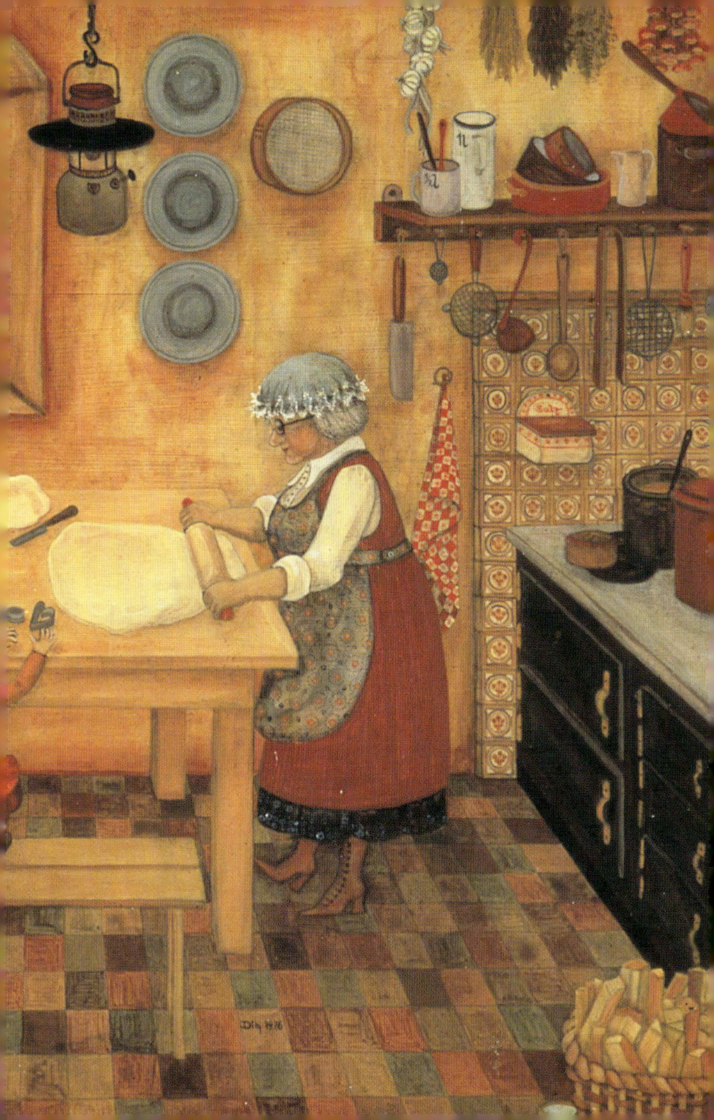

Marie-Thérèse, who married
Louis XIV of France in 1660, presented her fiancé with
chocolate in an ornate casket as an engagement
present. It was said of her that 'chocolate and the King
are her only passions'.

Whenever you want to have a really good
cup of chocolate, make it the day before,
in a porcelain coffeepot, and let it set.
The night's rest will concentrate it and give it a
velvety quality which will make it better.

Madame d'Arestel

Chocolate occasions the vapours,
and palpitation of the heart.

Madame de Sevigné

SWEET BLISS – A CARAMET!

Creamy caramel. Delicious milk chocolate – (Fry's of course).
Blending together in perfect bliss. Not too hard.
Not too soft. Not too big. Not too small. And with sixteen for
every sixpence, what a lot to share! Buy some TODAY.

NOW 16 for 6ᴰ Also 3ᵈ pack

CORONATION DAY
JUNE 26TH 1902
FRY'S
PURE SOLUBLE
BREAKFAST
COCOA
J.S. FRY & SONS, LTD
MADE BY
FRY'S
OINTMENT
"SAFETY" BRAND
SELECTED
STEEL PENS
BEST QUALITY.
G
M
Coronation of
KING GEORGE. V.
AND
QUEEN MARY
1911
UrillaC
POST FREE
REGAL
TRADE MARK
LOUD TONE
NEEDLES
200
200
DR RUMNEY'S
MENTHOLYPTUS
TOBACCO
PURE
SNUFF
BOURNVILLE
COCOA
MADE BY
Cadbury
TRADE MARK
PLAYER'S
NAVY CUT.
Gold Leaf
CIGARETTES
OXO
BRAND FLUID BEEF
IN CUBES

When you have breakfasted well and fully, if you will drink a big cup of chocolate at the end you will have digested the whole perfectly three hours later, and you will still be able to dine.

J. A. Brillat-Savarin, *La Physiologie du goût*

Chocolate is yummy and I know it's not good for you. Just eat it!

Charlie, 6

In 1675 Charles II issued a Proclamation for the Suppression of establishments serving chocolate, but it proved unenforceable and was forgotten in a matter of days.

Joseph Fry of Bristol, England, made the first eating chocolate in 1848 when he combined cocoa butter with chocolate liquor and sugar.

The Swiss prefer a very tender, melting chocolate, but the Germans, Europe's number two chocolate fanciers, go more for the bittersweet dark chocolate, along with the Danes and the French. Italians, Swedes and Finns prefer sweet chocolate. Chocolate in a blue wrapper won't sell in Shanghai or Hong Kong because the Chinese associate blue with death. Neither Swiss nor Germans like girl pictures on their chocolate packages, but want a realistic reproduction of the contents.

Nika Standen Hazelton

Those who wish for pure cocoa in all its quintessence
Will certainly find it in Cadbury's Essence.

Cadbury's advertisement, 1866

Chocolate is not only pleasant to taste, but it is a veritable balm of the mouth, for the maintaining of all glands and humours in a good state of health. Thus it is that all who drink it, possess a sweet breath.

Dr S. Blancardi

THE LITTLE BOOK OF CHOCOLATE

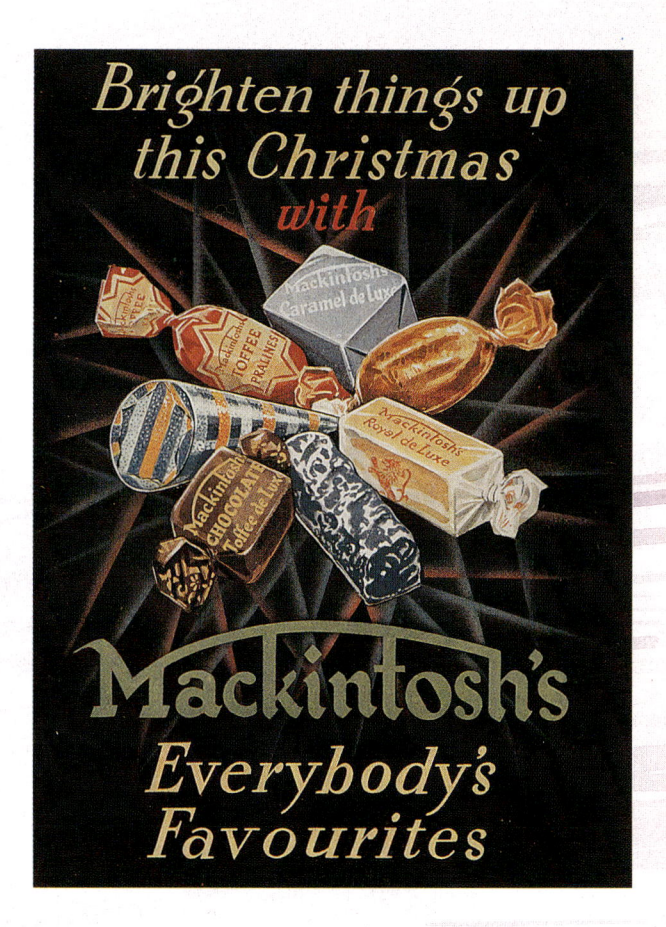

White Chocolate Truffles

150g white chocolate
65g unsalted butter
3 tbs double cream

Stir all ingredients together over a gentle heat, preferably using a double saucepan. Leave mixture in fridge for about 2 hours, then roll into balls and coat in cocoa powder, icing sugar, or desiccated coconut. The mixture softens very quickly, so it is best to keep the truffles in the fridge.

Chocolate is a quick-energy food, containing protein, fat, carbohydrate, calcium, phosphorus, iron, sodium, potassium, Vitamin A, thiamine, riboflavin and niacin.

What you see before you is the result of
a lifetime of chocolate.

Katharine Hepburn on her figure

The chocolate bar is an edible American flag, a security blanket for the distraught, a barometer of a nation's economic health.

New York Times, 25 February 1979

Caramels are a fad: chocolate is a permanent thing.

Milton Snavely Hershey

GIVE CHOCOLATES

The Chocolates I like Best

Rowntree's are the Chocolates of *guaranteed quality*. Every fancy box of Rowntree's Chocolates has the name of the Assortment inside the box clearly marked on the outside, thus guaranteeing the quality of the Chocolates within. Rowntree's have produced a splendid variety of fancy boxes this year.

All boxes containing 1 lb. or more of the well-known Rowntree's "York" Chocolates are sold at the price of the chocolates inside, no extra charge whatever being made for the box.

There are many assortments of Rowntree's Chocolates in beautiful fancy boxes from 1/- to 45/-.

Splendid Variety.

Full Value in the Chocolates.

ROWNTREE'S YORK CHOCOLATES
IN SPECIAL FANCY BOXES

THEY'RE RIGHT – IF THEY'RE ROWNTREE'S

Austrian militiamen and conscripts in the Second World War were known as chocolate soldiers.

Chocolate has been included in the foods provided on all American and Russian space flights because it is a morale booster that also provides nutrients.

Prisoners of the Aztecs were given chocolate to drink, because it was thought it would turn their hearts to chocolate.

When chocolate was first used in cooking it was added to savoury dishes. Recipes still exist today for turkey in chilli and chocolate sauce, duck with chocolate, chilli con carne with chocolate, wild boar in chocolate sauce and braised pigeon with chocolate.

The Swedish naturalist Carl Linnaeus gave the
cocoa tree its official name *Theobroma cacao*,
'food of the gods'.

Chocolate is the best thing in the world to eat.
Anne, 6

The persons who habitually take chocolate are those
who enjoy the most equable and constant health.
J. A. Brillat-Savarin, *La Physiologie du goût*

Samuel Pepys celebrated the coronation of Charles II
rather too well, and woke the following morning with a
terrible hangover. He recorded in his diary that he took
a cup of chocolate 'to settle my stomach'.

What use are cartridges in battle?
I always carry chocolate instead.
George Bernard Shaw, *Arms and the Man*

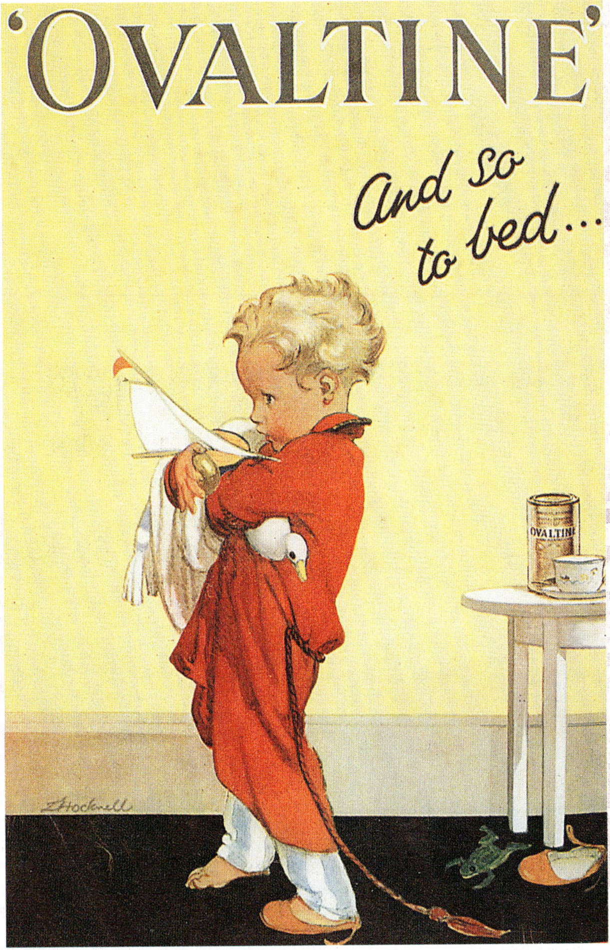
'OVALTINE'
And so to bed...
OVALTINE
J. Hockrell

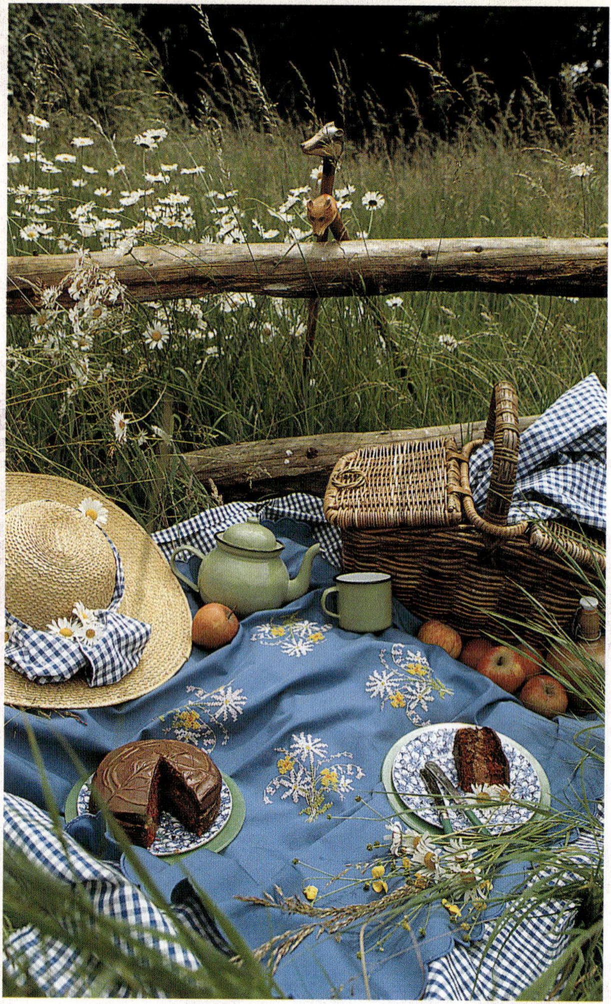

Just before serving a cup of hot chocolate,
top each cupful with a spoonful of whipped cream
and sprinkle with a little drinking chocolate,
sieved cocoa, cinnamon or nutmeg.

Life without chocolate
is lacking something important.
M. C. Morton

In the USA, each year several hundred thousand
Americans attend chocolate weekends.
Dances are held at which people dress up as their
favourite chocolate. At one such dance,
held at Miami's Fontainebleau Hilton Hotel, guests
were offered an opportunity to dunk actor Don
Johnson into a huge 2,700-litre
tank of chocolate syrup ...

THE LITTLE BOOK OF CHOCOLATE

Chocolate is madness; chocolate is delight.
Judith Olney

For supper I took a cup of hot chocolate at La Coupole.
I was fond of hot chocolate ...
Simone de Beauvoir

You are a very poor soldier: a chocolate cream soldier!
George Bernard Shaw, *Arms and the Man*

Since both its national products, snow and chocolate melt, the cuckoo clock was invented solely in order to give tourists something solid to remember it [Switzerland] by.
Alan Coren, *The Sanity Inspector*

Venice is like eating an entire box of chocolate liqueurs at one go.
Truman Capote

17,000 people today in Belgium
— that's one in every 200 workers —
are involved in the making,
selling and promotion of chocolate.

Chocolate truffles, both rich and light — ambrosia!
Anonymous

Does the notion of chocolate preclude
the concept of free will?
Sandra Boynton

Nine out of ten people like chocolate.
The tenth person always lies.
J. G. Tullius

I love chocolate because it makes me mad
because it has too much sugar.
Andrew, 6

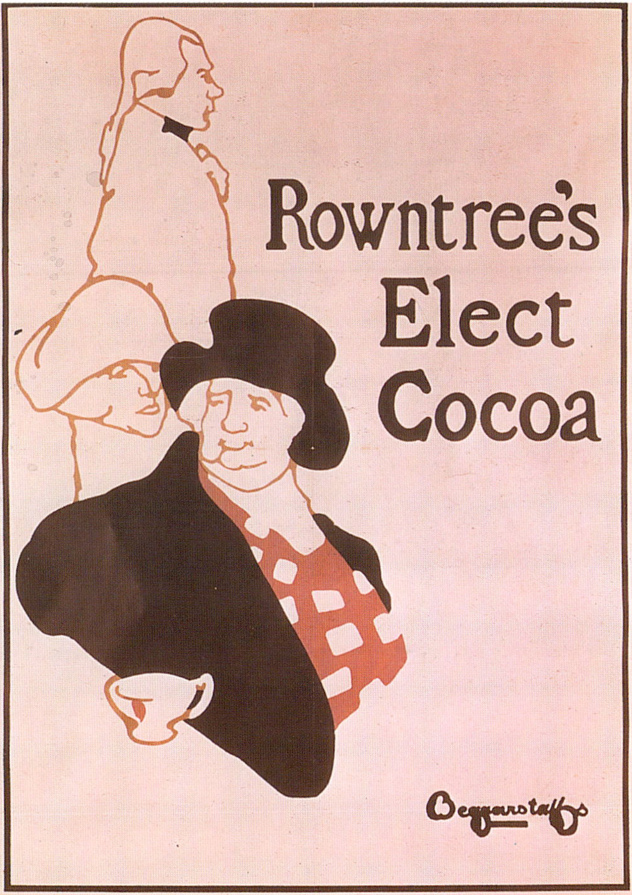
Rowntree's
Elect
Cocoa
Beggarstaffs

Chocolate Truffles

85g plain chocolate

1 egg yolk

15g butter

1 tsp rum

1 tsp cream

Melt chocolate over hot water.
Add the egg yolk, butter, rum and cream.
Beat until thick then chill
until firm enough to handle.
Form mixture into balls and toss at once in
chocolate vermicelli, cocoa powder or drinking
chocolate to coat.

As a wag at a bar once said to me,
'The explorer [Columbus] did not discover America,
he discovered chocolate.
And then God created the fritters.'

Tunku Varadarajan

It is believed that the word 'chocolate'
derives from the Mexican language:
'choco', a sound or noise, and 'atl', water,
because the Mexican people beat it in water
to make it foam.

Alexandre Dumas

Uno, dos, tres, cho –
Uno, dos, tres, – co –
Uno, dos, tres, – la –
Uno, dos, tres, – te
Bate, bate chocolate

Traditional Spanish rhyme

Everybody's Favourite
Quality itself
Mackintosh's
18 VARIETIES
TOFFEES CHOCOLATES BUTTER SCOTCH ETC – ETC
EVERY TIN A CHRISTMAS CARNIVAL IN ITSELF
Christmas Assortment de Luxe

The legendary lover Casanova
claimed that chocolate was more effective than
champagne for inducing romance.

The biggest chocolate sculpture ever made was a
4,484lb, 10-foot-high Easter egg, constructed in
Melbourne, Australia.

It has been shown as proof positive that carefully
prepared chocolate is ... above all helpful to people who
must do a great deal of mental work.

J. A. Brillat-Savarin, *La Physiologie du goût*

We have never believed anyone should have to wait
until the sun is high in the heavens to begin
enjoying chocolate.

Mary Goodbody

The superiority of chocolate drink,
both for health and nourishment,
will soon give it the same preference over
tea and coffee in America which it has in Spain.

Thomas Jefferson in a letter to John Adams, 1785

After the morning's cup of lilac chocolate,
I would hurry back to my quarters. ...
In Paris I was never hungry!

Colette

I would like to be presented with a beautiful red-headed young woman in the nude who is covered with a thick layer of chocolate. I then remove the chocolate as any red-blooded chocoholic male would.

Isaac Asimov

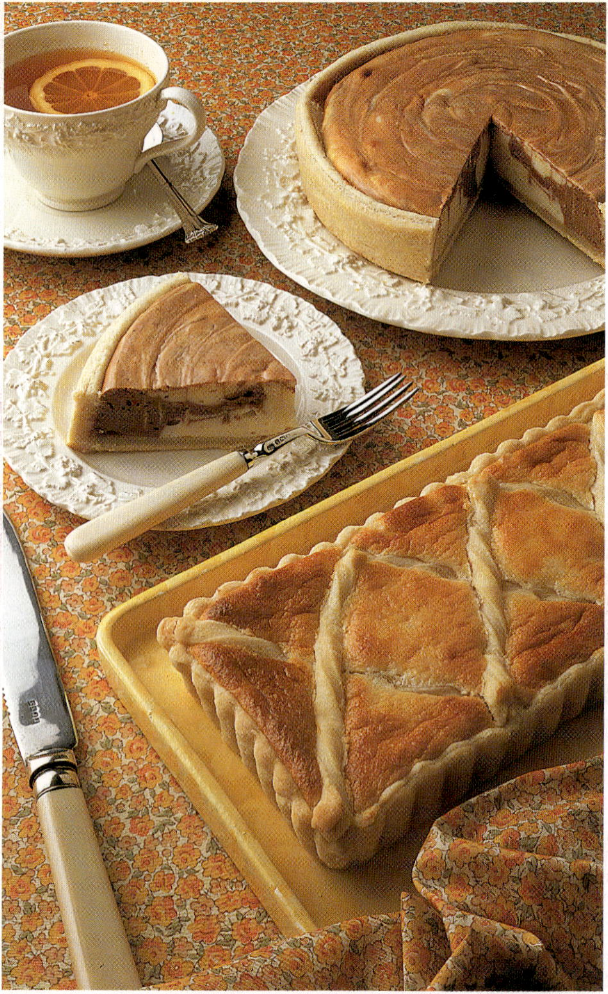

> i
> love
> you so
> i
> want
> to
> marry
> you
> and
> live
> forever
> in the
> flavour
> of your
> brown

Arnold Adoff, 'Chocolate, Chocolate'

I'm everyone's adorable and witty grandma and I live on chocolates and impossible coddling.

Katharine Hepburn

The world's favourite flavour.
No other flavour has ever rivalled chocolate in
universal appeal.

Mable Hoffman, *Chocolate Cookery*

What food do you crave?
Ask the question with enough smouldering emphasis
on the last word, and the answer is
bound to be chocolate.

Diane Ackerman

Chocolate stands in a class by itself and as such
deserves unabashed admiration.

Mary Goodbody and Brooke Dojny, *The Best of Chocolate*

It flatters you for a while;
it warms you for an instant;
then all of a sudden,
it kindles a mortal fever in you.

Madame de Sevigné

ESTABLISHED IN 1780
W. BAKER & Co.
DORCHESTER MASS.
Manufacturers
CHOCOLATE,
COCOA,
BROMA
AND
COCOA PASTE.
HOMŒOPATHIC
AND
DIETETIC COCOA
These articles are manufactured from Cocoa of the best kind and quality, and are warranted equal, if not superior to any other CHOCOLATE made in the United States & may be returned if found unequal to the recommendation.
BOSTON, MASS.

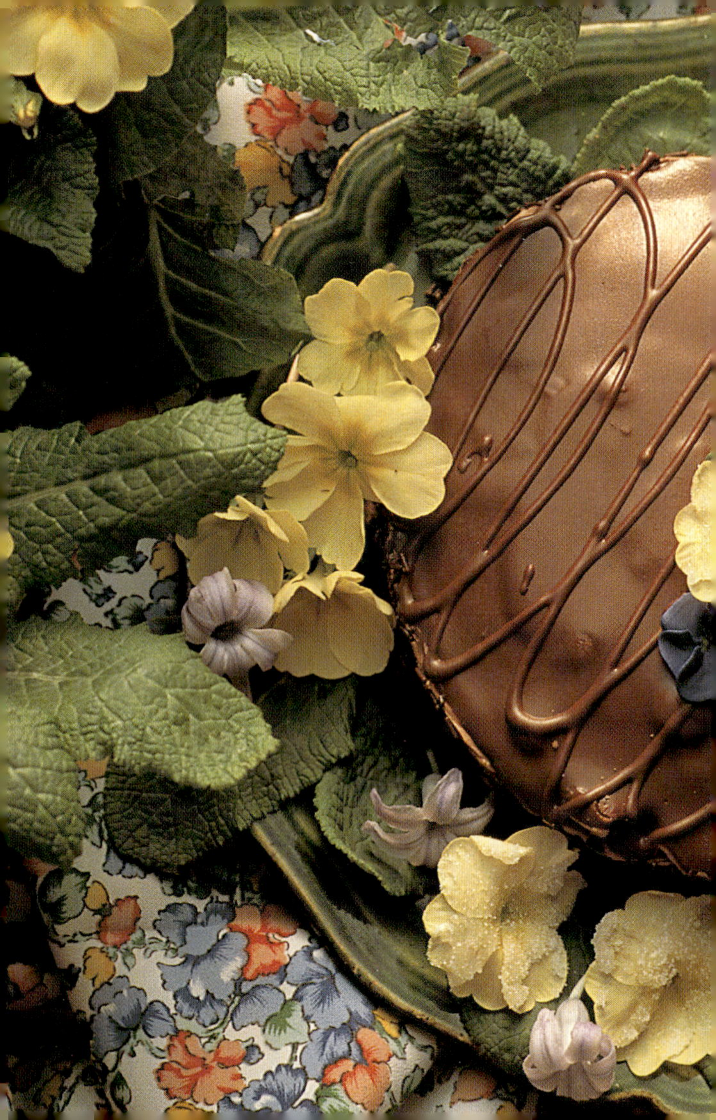

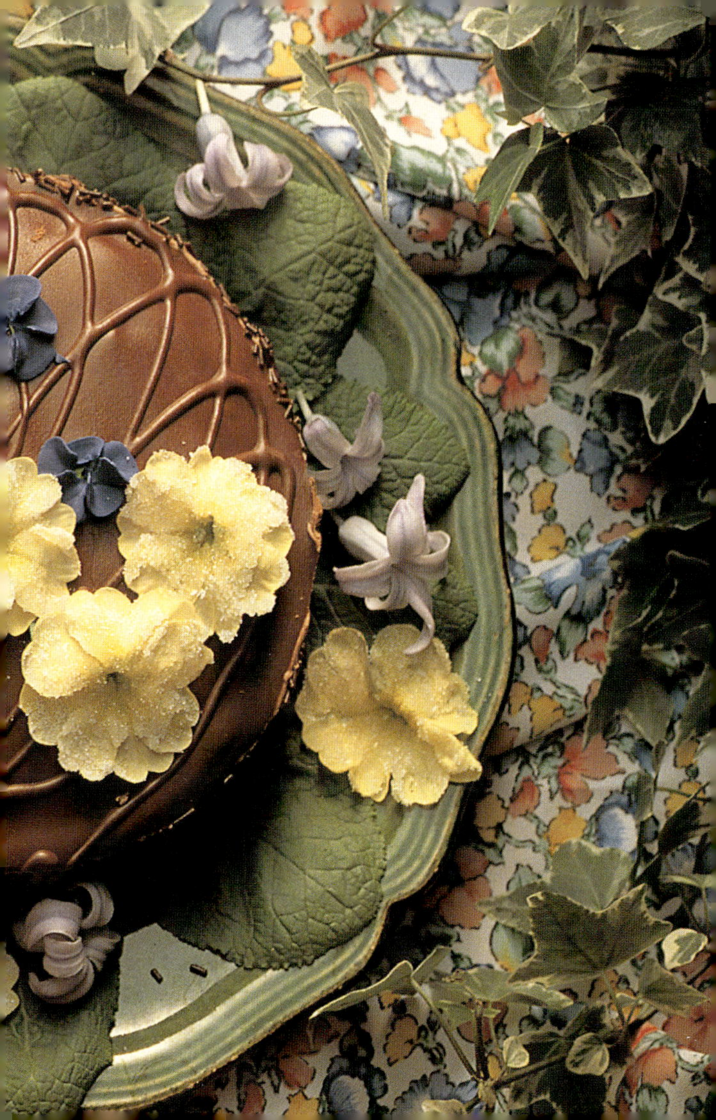

Chocolate Cake

Look — no eggs!

150g plain flour
30g cocoa
1 tsp bicarbonate of soda
200g sugar
pinch salt
240ml water
80ml vegetable oil
2 tsp vanilla essence
1 tbs vinegar

Sift dry ingredients and whisk in everything else. Divide between two or three greased and floured sandwich tins. Bake at 160°C/320°F/gas mark 3 for 20-25 minutes. Leave in pans for 10 minutes before turning out.

"The Charm of Flavour"

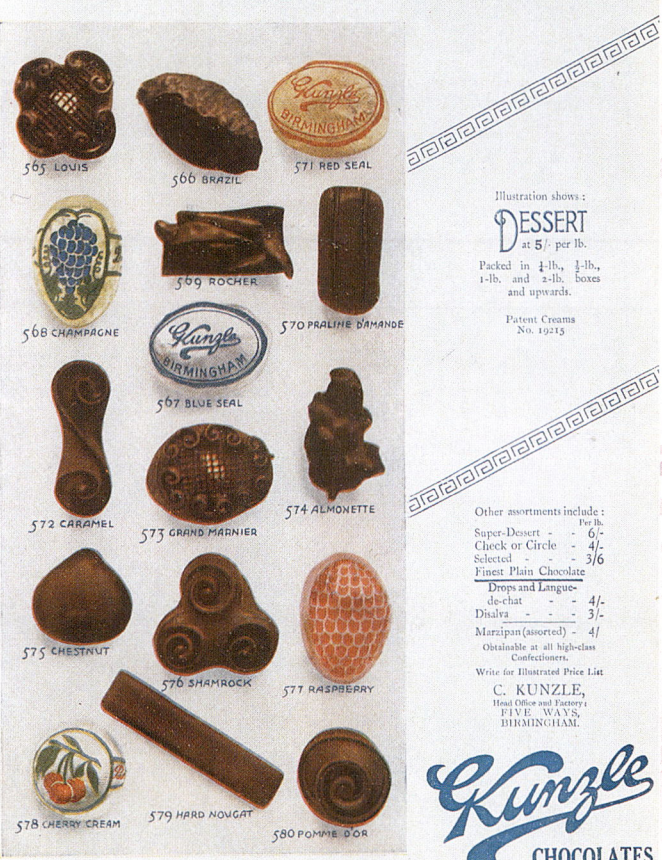

565 LOUIS
566 BRAZIL
571 RED SEAL
568 CHAMPAGNE
569 ROCHER
570 PRALINE D'AMANDE
567 BLUE SEAL
572 CARAMEL
573 GRAND MARNIER
574 ALMONETTE
575 CHESTNUT
576 SHAMROCK
577 RASPBERRY
578 CHERRY CREAM
579 HARD NOUGAT
580 POMME D'OR

Illustration shows:

DESSERT
at **5/-** per lb.

Packed in ¼-lb., ½-lb., 1-lb. and 2-lb. boxes and upwards.

Patent Creams
No. 19215

Other assortments include:
Per lb.
Super-Dessert - - 6/-
Check or Circle - 4/-
Selected - - - 3/6
Finest Plain Chocolate
Drops and Langue-
de-chat - - - 4/-
Disalva - - - 3/-
Marzipan (assorted) 4/

Obtainable at all high-class Confectioners.

Write for Illustrated Price List.

C. KUNZLE,
Head Office and Factory:
FIVE WAYS,
BIRMINGHAM.

Kunzle
CHOCOLATES
(MADE IN BIRMINGHAM)
LONDON & BIRMINGHAM

London Office and Showrooms:
19, CHARING CROSS ROAD,
W.C. 2
(next to Alhambra)

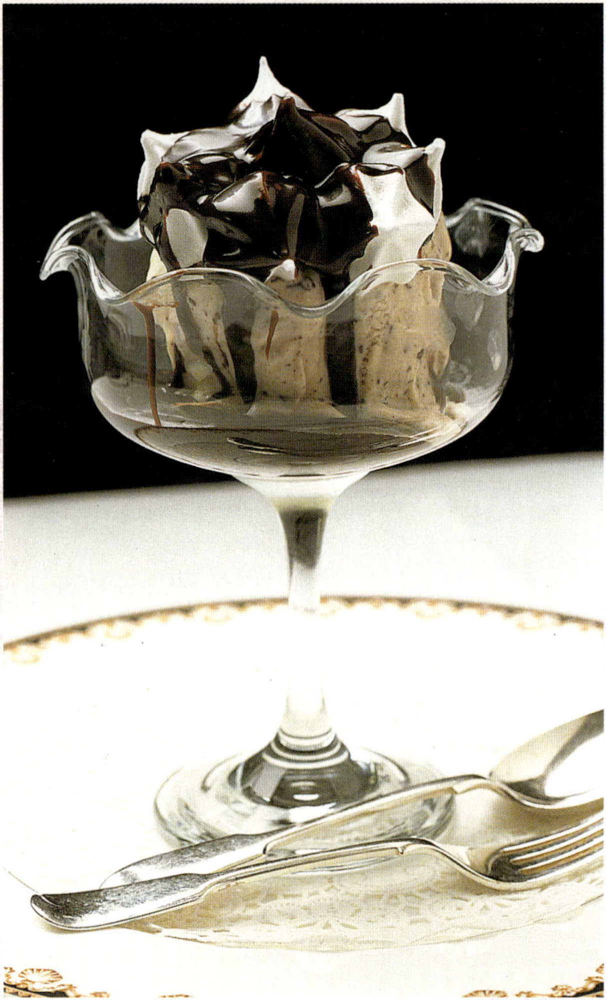

Chocolate Sauce

250ml strong black coffee
2 heaped tbs cocoa
4 heaped tbs sugar
25g butter

Boil all ingredients together until reduced
and thick – delicious!

It's a sin, wickedly rich and fattening,
but every spoonful is glory, and that's what
chocolate mousse is supposed to be.

Julia Child

In 1875 Daniel Peter of Switzerland added
condensed milk to chocolate to produce
the first solid milk chocolate bar.

According to Chocosuisse, the trade association of
Swiss chocolate companies, the following are
the characteristics of good chocolate:

— an unblemished, silky sheen

— breaks off firmly and crisply with clean edges,
and without crumbling

— a full and rounded, yet unobtrusive aroma

— melts like butter in the mouth;
doesn't feel gritty on the tongue or stick to the palate

— a fine, delicate and unique flavour.

Chocophile — a person who loves chocolate.
Chocoholic — a person who loves, really loves,
chocolate.

Chocolate Mousse

150g plain chocolate
2 tsp instant coffee powder
3 eggs, separated
3 tbs Tia Maria
150ml double cream

Melt the chocolate over a pan of hot water. Beat in the coffee powder, egg yolks and liqueur. Remove from heat and allow to cool. Whip cream until thick and fold through chocolate mixture. Beat the egg whites till stiff, then fold into chocolate mixture. Chill, though not overnight, and decorate with whipped cream just before serving.

THE LITTLE BOOK OF CHOCOLATE

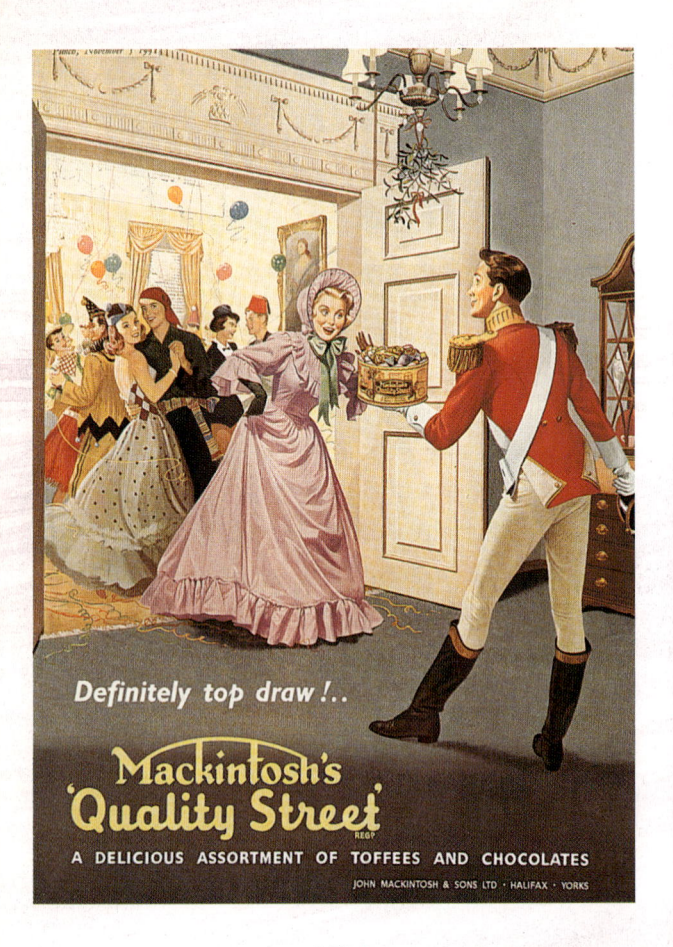

Definitely top draw!..

Mackintosh's 'Quality Street'

A DELICIOUS ASSORTMENT OF TOFFEES AND CHOCOLATES

JOHN MACKINTOSH & SONS LTD · HALIFAX · YORKS

Chocolate Fudge

450g sugar
150ml milk
150g butter
150g plain chocolate
50g honey

Lightly oil a shallow 16cm square tin.
Heat all ingredients gently in a large heavy saucepan, stirring until the sugar has dissolved. Bring to the boil, then continue boiling until a temperature of
115°C/240°F has been reached,
stirring only occasionally to prevent sticking.
Remove pan from heat and stand on a cool surface for 5 minutes, then beat the mixture until thick, creamy and beginning to 'grain'. Pour into prepared tin, and mark into squares when almost set.
Cut when cold.

The divine drink,
which builds up resistance and fights fatigue.
A cup of this precious drink permits a man to
walk for a whole day without food.

Montezuma, Aztec Emperor

True chocovores are matutinal creatures:
they rise, shower and then hit the sweet, sticky brown
stuff which gives them fuel for the day.

Tunku Varadarajan

Other things are just food.
But chocolate's chocolate.

Patrick Skene Catling

One chocolate chip provides enough food
energy for an adult to walk 150 feet.
Therefore it takes about 35 chocolate chips
to move you a mile, or 875,000 to get you
around the world.

THE LITTLE BOOK OF CHOCOLATE

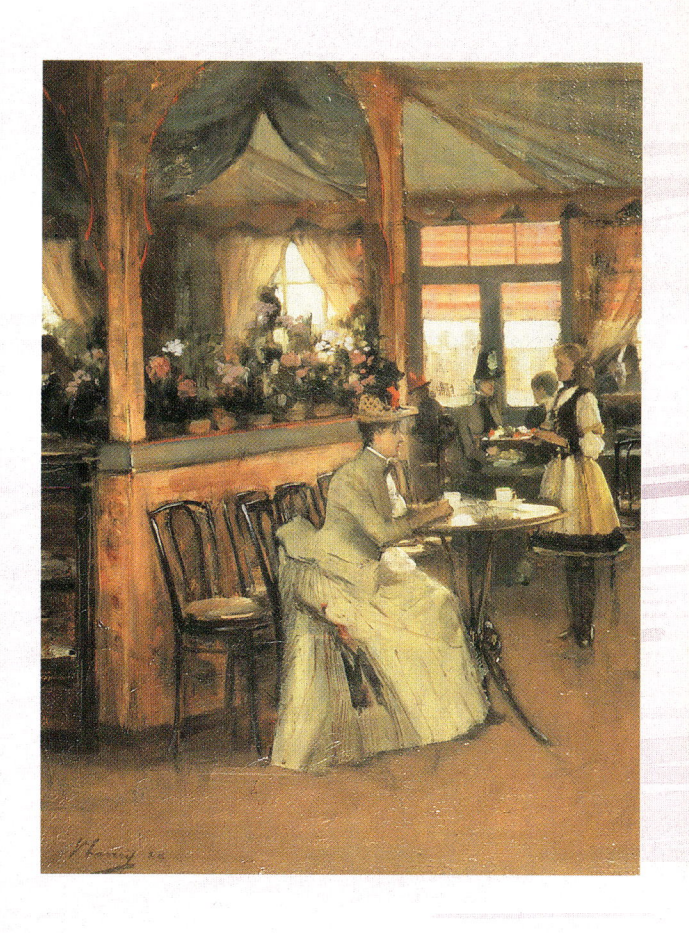

It is nice.
It is messy.
It is brown.

Tom, 6

Ten thousand million Smarties are consumed
annually in the UK.

... the taste of chocolate
is a sensual pleasure in itself,
existing in the same world as sex ...
For myself, I can enjoy the wicked pleasure
of chocolate ... entirely by myself.
Furtiveness makes it better.

Dr Ruth (Westheimer)

When people give me surprises,
they usually give me chocolate.

Hannah, 4

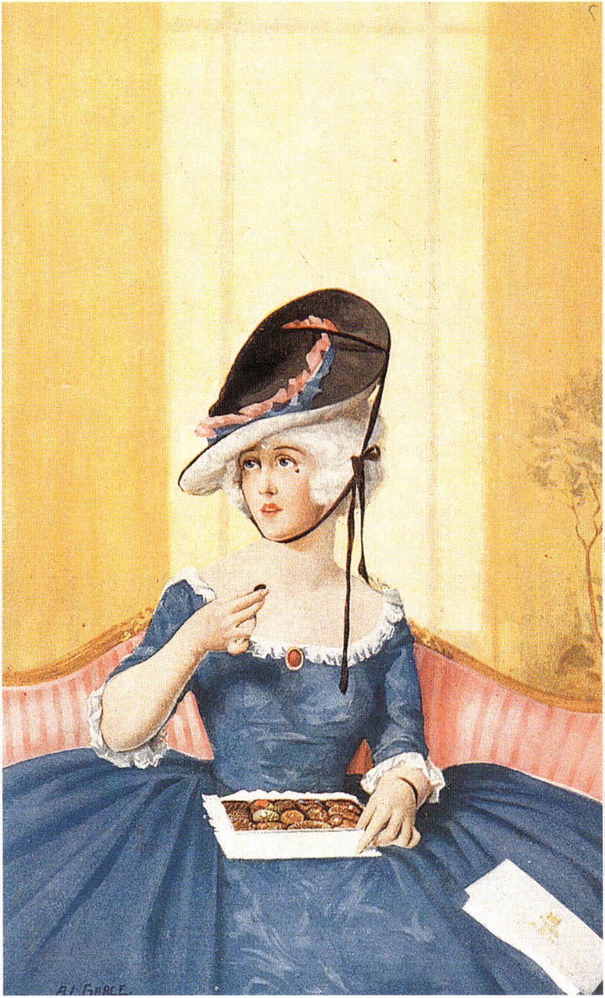

Chocolate Chip and Macadamia Nut Cookies

75g butter or margarine, softened
75g granulated sugar
75g light brown soft sugar
1 tsp vanilla essence
1 egg beaten
175g self-raising flour
pinch salt
125g chocolate drops
75g macadamia nuts, roughly chopped

Cream the butter until very soft.
Gradually beat in the sugars and vanilla essence.

Add the beaten egg and mix well.
Sift the flour and salt into a bowl. Fold carefully through the creamed mixture. Add the chocolate drops and 50g of the nuts. Stir to mix.

Roll the mixture into small balls. Place on greased baking sheets, leaving space for spreading, and flatten lightly with a wet fork. Sprinkle on remaining nuts, pressing them down lightly.

Bake at 180°C/350°F/gas mark 4 for about 10 minutes or until pale gold in colour.
Remove from oven and put on wire rack to cool slightly. These are best eaten warm.

Chocolate cake
Chocolate cake
that's the one
I'll help you make
flour, soda
salt are sifted
butter sugar
cocoa lifted
by the eggs
then mix the whole
grease the pans
I'll lick the bowl
chocolate caked
chocolate caked
that's what I'll be
when it's baked.

Nina Payne, *Chocolate Cake*

Notes on Illustrations

Page 5 *Chocolate Cake with Flowers.* Courtesy of Elizabeth Whiting & Associates, London; **Page 6-7** *Box of Cadbury's Assorted Chocolates* (Private Collection). Courtesy of The Bridgeman Art Library; **Page 9** *Chocolates & Coo Poems.* Courtesy of The Laurel Clark Collection; **Page 10** *Give Chocolates this Season. They're Right – If They're Rowntree's* (The Sketch Christmas Number, 1924). Courtesy of The Laurel Clark Collection; **Page 13** Tesco, *Cheesecakes –Luxury Chocolate Cheesecake,* Martin Brigdalf. Courtesy of Reed Consumer Books; **Page 14-15** *Biscuit Baking Day,* Ditz (Private Collection). Courtesy of The Bridgeman Art Library. **Page 17** *Sweet Bliss – A Caramel!* Courtesy of The Laurel Clark Collection; **Page 18** *Selection of Brand Tins,* (Private Collection). Courtesy of The Bridgeman Art Library; **Page 21** *Brighten Things this Christmas with Mackintosh's – Everybody's Favourites.* Courtesy of The Laurel Clark Collection; **Page 23** Sainsbury, *Chocolate Cooking,* Paul Williams. Courtesy of Reed Consumer Books; **Page 24** *Give Chocolates – They're Right – If They're Rowntree's.* Courtesy of The Laurel Clark Collection; **Page 27** *"Ovaltine' And so to bed ...* Courtesy of The Laurel Clark Collection; **Page 28** *Picnic with Hat and Basket.* Courtesy of Elizabeth Whiting & Associates, London; **Page 30** *White Heather for Me! It's Such a Colourful Assortment.* Courtesy of The Laurel Clark Collection; **Page 33** *Rowntrees Elect Cocoa* (Private Collection). Courtesy of The Bridgeman Art Library; **Page 34-5** *Chocolate Truffles.* Courtesy of Elizabeth Whiting & Associates, London; **Page 37** *Mackintosh's Christmas Assortment de Luxe* (The Strand Magazine). Courtesy of The Laurel Clark Collection; **Page 40** Tesco, *Cheesecakes-Marbled Cheesecake; Cinnamon Apple Cheesecake,* Martin Brigdale. Courtesy of Reed Consumer Books; **Page 43** *American Advertising Poster for Chocolate and Other Cocoa Products* (Private Collection). Courtesy of The Bridgeman Art Library; **Page 44-5** *Chocolate Cake with Flowers.* Courtesy of Elizabeth Whiting & Associates, London; **Page 46** *The Charm of Flavour – Kunzle Chocolates.* Courtesy of The Laurel Clark Collection; **Page 48** *Chocolate Sauce.* Courtesy of Elizabeth Whiting & Associates, London; **Page 51** *Go On – Spoil Yourself! – Fry's Chocolate Cream.* Courtesy of The Laurel Clark Collection; **Page 52** *Definitely Top Draw! 'Quality Street'.* Courtesy of The Laurel Clark Collection; **Page 55** *A Cup of Chocolate,* Sir John Lavery (Whitford & Hughes, London). Courtesy of The Bridgeman Art Library; **Page 57** *Maison Lyons Chocolates Bring Consolation.* Courtesy of The Laurel Clark Collection.

Acknowledgements: The Publishers wish to thank everyone who gave permission to reproduce the quotes in this book. Every effort has been made to contact the copyright holders, but in the event that an oversight has occurred, the publishers would be delighted to rectify any omissions in future editions of this book. Children's quotes printed courtesy of Herne Hill School; recipes supplied by Deborah Gill; *The Secret Chocolate Lover's Handbook,* Caroline Archer, reprinted courtesy of Red Fox, a division of Random House UK Limited; *Chocolate, Chocolate,* Arnold Adoff; *Chocolate Cake,* Nina Payne, reprinted courtesy of the author.